A CENTURY *of*
DUNFERMLINE

In the 1960s many long-standing businesses were still in operation in Bruce Street, including Pickfords' and Stevenson's salerooms. *(DCL)*

A CENTURY *of* DUNFERMLINE

BRUCE DURIE

WHSmith

First published in the United Kingdom in 2002 by
Sutton Publishing Limited exclusively for
WHSmith, Greenbridge Road, Swindon SN3 3LD

British Library Cataloguing in Publication Data
A catalogue record for this book is available from the British Library.

ISBN 0-7509-3137-X

Illustrations

Front endpaper: Aerial view of Dunfermline, 1936. *(DCL)*
Back endpaper: Aerial view of Dunfermline, 1981. *(DCL)*
Half title page: Aerial view of the palace and park, 1967. *(DCL)*
Title page: This engraving by R. Scott for the *Scots Magazine* of April 1810 shows Dunfermline from a position roughly that of the railway station today. *(DCL)*

Typeset in 11/14pt Photina and produced by
Sutton Publishing Limited, Phoenix Mill,
Thrupp, Stroud, Gloucestershire GL5 2BU.
Printed and bound in England by
J.H. Haynes & Co. Ltd, Sparkford.

Contents

Is it fair to assume that all nine of this family lived in the same house in North Inglis Street in 1900? *(DCL)*

Introduction

In a way, the story of Dunfermline is easy to tell – capital of medieval Scotland, home to coal-mining monks, adopted abode of a saint, burial place of kings, ecclesiastical centre until the Reformation, hub of the weaving industry, a royal burgh and later a city, recipient of Carnegie benefice, site of crucial naval defences and dockyards, neglected industrial backwater, fast-growing commuter town, nexus of the digital revolution. However, the real story is much more complex – and far more interesting. The twists and skeins of history that thread through Dunfermline toun binding the warp of human lives to the weft of events are more intricate than any book can hope to reflect. In the end the story of a place is the story of the people who lived in it once and live in it still. But by reminding them of places they can no longer see and things they have almost forgotten, they can carry the story forward, and a little less may be lost.

EARLIEST DAYS

Before the mid-eleventh century there is not much by way of reliable historical narrative about the area. The Dark Ages remain stubbornly dark. But the importance assumed by Dunfermline around the time of King Malcolm III (Malcolm Canmore, 1057/8–93) means that it is well documented from then on. Most histories of the town start from this point, as if Dunfermline were uninhabited until a king chose to build a tower there. However, another story is told by the surviving place names from the time of the Roman occupation (AD 83–440) and the subsequent Dark Ages.

For almost 400 years this was more or less the northern edge of the Roman Empire – the Antonine Wall, constructed in about AD 142, stretches for 40 miles from Bo'ness across the Forth to Old Kilpatrick near Glasgow. The Romans' tenuous grip on this savage land was maintained by strongholds at a Praetorium (later called Praetor Hill and today Prate-house, 3 miles east of Dunfermline), supported by camps at Lochore a few miles north and at Carnock to the west. Pictish and Celtic names have survived from before the Roman occupation. The word *bal* (a dwelling) is found in Balmule, Balyeomen and Balclune; the prefix *caer* (a castle) is in Carnock (*Caer-knoc*), Carniehill and Keirsbeath; the Celto-British word *pit* is common in the area, as in Pittencrieff, Pitfirrane, Pitscottie and Pitreavie; and the Celtic *dun* (a hill fort) survives in Dunduff, Donibristle, Dunearn and Dunfermline itself.

The Roman name for the town, Mons Infirmorum, was used in the Latin charter of Malcolm III which founded the abbey. But the original name, Dunfermline, which supplanted it, possibly derives from the Celtic *dun* (fortified hill), *fiaram* (bent or crooked) and *lin* (a cascade or pool). The rivulet around the base of the Tower Hill is certainly crooked and plummets over the 15-foot cascade of the Ferm burn (now called the Glen Falls, see page 69).

The earliest reference to the name is in the Confirmation Charters of David I around 1128 where it appears as Dunfermelitane and the next year as Dunfermelin. Early seals and badges (page 12) clearly refer to Dunfermline. By 1690, it had been fixed as Dunfermline, although some rather whimsical Latin forms such as Dunum Fermelinum and Fermilodunum were used around this time and for a century or so after.

SEALS OF THE ABBEY AND BOROUGH of DUNFERMLINE.

PLATE III.

Supposed about Ann. 1300.

About Ann: 1200.

Borough Seal

George Dury Abbot & Commendator 1539-1560

Abbot Radulph about Ann: 1292.

Abbot Patrick about Ann: 1185.

The abbey seal of about 1300 (top left) and the burgh seal below it show fanciful representations of Malcolm's Tower. The seal of Abbot George Durie is notable for omitting it, including instead references to St Andrew and his own family's coat of arms. Earlier abbots (bottom) had been humbler. *(DCL)*

THE CULDEES AT DUNFERMLINE

Dunfermline appears to have been an important centre of the Celtic church, and in particular of the Culdees. There is a great deal of fanciful speculation about this loose confederation of non-celibate monks – but from at least 570 they do seem to have had settlements at Dunfermline and other places nearby: Kirkcaldy (*Caer Culdea*), Abernethy, Balchristie, Bolgin, Culross, Kirkheugh (St Andrews), Loch Leven, Portmoak, Pittenweem, and on Inchcolm and the Isle of May in the Firth of Forth. Their church in Dunfermline would have been small and primitive in structure – intended for about fifty brothers – and probably situated on or near the later abbey grounds. We can only speculate, but Queen Margaret's known desire to suppress the Culdees in favour of her Catholic faith may have led to the complete obliteration of the Dunfermline and other Culdee churches. No real sign of it remains today.

THE ARRIVAL OF MARGARET

Legend has it that sometime between 1067 and 1070 Edgar the Ætheling, deprived of succession to the English throne, together with his mother Agatha, his sisters Margaret and Christian, and a retinue, set out from Hungary, where they had lived for safety during their childhood. A violent storm drove them into the Firth of Forth and they were wrecked on the northern shore near the castle of the king of Scots. When King Malcolm heard of their arrival he left Dunfermline and rushed to their aid. Finding them alive and well, he received them cordially, invited them to take his hospitality and fell in love with Princess Margaret, whom he married in 1069.

The more likely story strips away some of this fancy. Certainly Edmund Ironside, Saxon king of England, was murdered in 1016 or 1017 after his defeat by Canute's Danes. Edward the Exile, his eldest son, took shelter in Normandy then Hungary and there married a local noblewoman called Agatha, by whom he had Edgar and two daughters, Margaret and Christian. Edgar and his sisters returned to England in 1057 to advance their claim to the throne. Edward the Confessor neutralized this threat by raising the young Edgar in his court while Margaret, Christian and Agatha lived mostly in a nunnery for twelve years. Any aspirations Edgar might have had were thwarted by the Norman invasion in 1066. And, most importantly, in the autumn of 1069 when the ill-fated ship was supposedly driven ashore, Malcolm was not in Scotland. He was harrying Durham and the surrounding countryside. Edgar had just made his last unsuccessful foray against the Normans near York. He and his nearest relatives took ship for Monks Wearmouth where they met Malcolm and his army. Whether it was Malcolm's idea or Edgar's, the English prince and his family decided to sail immediately for Scotland and take up residence at Dunfermline, pending a later combined assault on England. The exiles set out at the end of October, and far from encountering rough weather they sailed before a favourable east wind and arrived safely near Malcolm's residence. In this light, the subsequent (and rather quick) marriage of the 47-year-old Malcolm to the 24-year-old Margaret must be seen as a dynastic alliance to secure both parties' interests. According to St Dunelm, Malcolm was betrothed to Margaret long before the marriage. The mythological features – the storm, the shipwreck and the fairy-tale love at first sight – were later embellishments intended to give the story a miraculous aspect.

Whatever the details of the story Margaret certainly lost no time in setting her stamp on the Scots. She brought the sophistication of her upbringing at the Hungarian court and as an Anglo-Saxon princess to the more primitive kingdom of Malcolm. She advanced her Roman Christianity at the expense of the Celtic Church. And she is reputed to have taught the Scots nobles to eat with knives

The remains of Malcolm Canmore's Tower in Pittencrieff Park. Supposedly the residence of Malcolm III before his marriage to Margaret in 1069–70, the tower sank from historical trace. Well fortified, standing on a high rocky protrusion (Montaculum – a little hill) surrounded by dense forest and set in a flat plain, it was easily defended and therefore a suitable stronghold for a warrior king. The site was cleared from 1884 and in 1905 and 1906 several finds were made of earthenware, kitchen debris, pieces of leather and a small cave which probably served as a fireplace or oven. *(DCL)*

instead of fingers and to wipe their hands on napkins rather than on their beards. Whether these nobles were really so primitive and resisted bathing and hand-washing is doubtful – many of them would have spoken Latin and even French – but Margaret's influence was certainly deeply felt. Malcolm founded a church for her and her favoured confessor and biographer Turgot. She in turn established a chapel in Edinburgh Castle, set up the Queen's Ferry to help pilgrims and others travel between Edinburgh and Dunfermline, and conducted many acts of piety and charity. According to Turgot (who had every reason to be a complete toady) Margaret prepared food each morning for nine orphans and fed them on her bended knee, ministered at table to the poor and washed the feet of six children every evening. Royal 'spin' was evident even in the eleventh century. However, Margaret does appear to have provided much-needed splendour at court. A snappy dresser herself, she set a fashion for colourful clothes. She also persuaded the king to have more attendants, encouraged him to make more frequent and more splendid public appearances, and had him served at table on silver and gold plate.

All of this might be fact, obsequiousness or public relations – at the time the 'illustrious exiles' and the large influx that followed them were regarded with suspicion in Scotland. On the other hand, it is certainly the case that Malcolm entrusted his queen with many matters regarding religion and some internal policies of his kingdom. She instigated strict observance of Sunday, administered the household, took charge of entertaining and more or less eradicated unseemly conduct. Malcolm, on the other hand, was courageous in battle but illiterate and had few other abilities. He was completely under her sway. No wonder his nobles regarded the English princess and the 'illustrious exiles' askance.

Malcolm died in 1093, seventy years of age, while besieging Alnwick (although some say he was murdered to allow Donald Bane to become king). Prince Edward – one of at least eight children – received a mortal wound and died days later. When Queen Margaret was told of their violent deaths by her youngest and favourite son, Ethelrede, she was on her sick bed in Edinburgh Castle. Years of strict religious observance and the ascetic life seem to have brought on consumption. This, added to her grief, was enough to sap her remaining strength and after making confession to Turgot and receiving the Holy Sacrament, she gave her blessing to all around her and died on 16 November 1093, in her forty-seventh year. At the time the castle was under siege by the usurper, Donald Bane. Ethelrede and the queen's attendants were forced to get Margaret's body out of the castle through a secret door, a mist shrouding their exit. The body was taken by the Queen's Ferry to Dunfermline and deposited before the Rwde Awtre (the Altar of the Holy Cross or Rood) with great veneration and honour.

THE ROYAL BURGH AND BURIAL PLACE OF KINGS

Alexander I made Dunfermline a royal burgh in 1109 or 1112. As the royal burial ground was the last resting place of his beloved mother Margaret and his brothers Edward and Edgar, in 1115 he arranged for his father Malcolm Canmore's remains to be exhumed from Tynemouth and laid in their intended sepulchre. He built the two towers and the grand entrance at the western end of the church, and established the monastery to service the church, which now had Abbey status.

By 1396 there were six ports or gates to Dunfermline. The ports were necessary for the protection of burgh rights and the levying of tolls and duties; they also provided a modicum of defence. These ports and their modern equivalents were: The Mill, or Collieraw Port (top of Bruce Street); Rottenraw Port (near the top of South Chapel Street); Crosswynd Port (now Crosswynd); East Port (east of High Street); Tolbooth Port (foot of Bruce Street); West Port (middle of St Catherine's Wynd). There may have been a seventh at the eastern end of Maygate. The burgh was no more than 1,000 yards around its perimeter. Tolls collected were taken to the burgh clerk in his tollbooth, which as in most Scottish towns also served as a prison. The Market Cross was erected about the same time.

Dunfermline remained capital of Scotland for the next forty years. However, by 1436, the year James I was murdered, Dunfermline, along with Perth, Stirling and Scone, was felt to have insufficient defences to protect royalty against the designs of the nobles. Edinburgh Castle was deemed a safer place of residence for the royal families. Edinburgh became Scotland's capital and Dunfermline was relegated to secondary status.

During the sixteenth century the main thoroughfares in Dunfermline took up their familiar configuration. They were called rows, gates, wynds, and vennels – there were no roads or streets then. The royal palace seems to have been enlarged and repaired about 1540, with mullioned windows and an upper storey added. In 1599 the Bailie's house and Serjeant's house were built by William Schaw, who also restored and added to the abbey and built Queen Anne's House. These tall houses were erected close to the west end of the Old Church as residences for the high constable, mayor and serjeant, and for the Heritable Bailie of the Regality of Dunfermline, a post created for David Durie by his cousin, Abbot George Durie, in 1580. He resigned his office into the hands of Queen Anne in 1596, who in 1611 conferred it on Alexander Seton, by then Earl of Dunfermline. The date-stone originally above one of the doors of these buildings is now above the gate of Pittencrieff policy.

George Durie was some piece of work. In some ways, he was the cause of the Reformation. Protestantism came late to Scotland – last of all the reformed European nations. Durie's uncle, James Beaton, had gathered to himself a great many prestigious offices, including archbishop of St Andrews at the same time as being abbot of Dunfermline. George was his successor as commendator (abbot) and also became an important politician, guardian to the infant Queen Mary and scourge of Protestants – he even had his own cousin John Durie, a monk at Dunfermline, walled up for 'heresy'. Such abuses fomented opposition and when the reformers marched on the abbey in 1560 to destroy it, Durie spirited away St Margaret's reliquary, an ornate casket containing her head and some bones, to the Jesuits in Antwerp and eventually to the Scots College in Douai, France. He fled to France himself and died in 1565. John Durie went on to be a noted preacher and reformer.

BIRTH OF A KING AND THE GREAT FIRE

Charles, second son of King James VI, was born in the royal palace on 19 November 1600 (as was a third son, Robert, in 1601; he lived only a few months). A legend tells that Charles's nurse let out a shriek one night, rousing the king. She claimed to have seen an old man near the baby's crib, putting a cloak over him. James, whose interest in demonology and all things hellish was well known, declared that once the Devil had cast a cloak over someone, no good would come of them and that 'gin he ever be King, there'll be nae gude i' his ring'. He was right, of course, Charles I being one of the worst monarchs ever foisted on Britain.

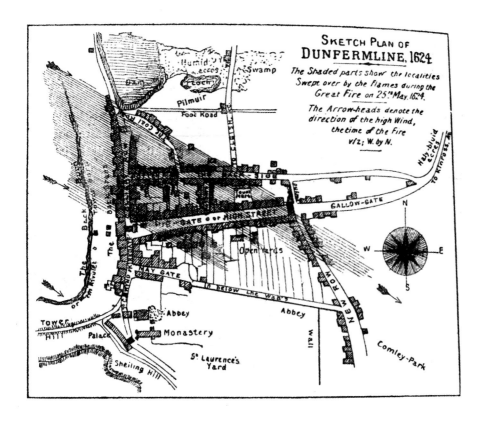

This 1624 map of Dunfermline shows the area affected by the great fire of that year. The blaze spread as far north as present-day Pilmuir Street, destroying the Grammar School, next to where the post office stands (page 50). Notice also the old street names – Hie Gate (High Street), Gallowgate, Back Rigs, In Below The Wa's, Rotten Row and Colliery Row. *(DCL)*

16

The Union in 1603 took James VI and I to England, ending Dunfermline's status as a royal palace of the kings of Scots (although James stayed there during his one and only visit to Scotland in 1617 and Queen Anne remained fond of Dunfermline).

A fire devastated the town on 25 May 1624. Strangely, there is no mention of this in the burgh records, although reports of it do appear in those of other burghs. This fire was accidental, caused by a bailie's son who fired a gun during the Wappinshaw Day drill. Burning wadding fell on the thatched or heather roof of a house near Rotten Row. It spread to other houses and three-quarters of the town was engulfed. The blaze was commemorated on a number of rebuilt or new houses. For example, at the north-west corner of Cross Wynd, a new house was erected or completed in 1626. Among numerous inscriptions on the 'Fire Stane' set high in the wall is a Latin biblical text which translates as: 'Seeing that in so brief a space, on the 25th May, 1624, so much desolation was caused by a fire and the fury of the flaming blast, then O consider the dreadful blazing pyres which the breath of Jehovah, as if with a torrent of brimstone, will for ever keep in flames.' (Isaiah xxx: 33) and the initials 'M.R.D.', referring to (Master) Robert Durie MA. Other stones found in the house during renovations in the mid-1800s bear the initials 'I.D.' (John Durie?) and the inscription 'M.W.D. A Fvndamento Denvo Extrvxit' ('Master. W.D. built this house new from the foundations'), presumably referring to another Durie, or to the mason or builder. These stones and others are now collected together at the west end of the abbey nave. A census taken in 1635, when the town had recovered somewhat, records 1,850 souls in Dunfermline and surrounds.

THE PALACE IN RUINS

Early in 1708, during a great snowstorm and frost, the north gable, part of the front wall and most of the roof of the palace fell in, leaving it the utter ruin it remains today. The abbey was faring no better. At the start of the eighteenth century the old nave was still being used as a parish kirk (the only kirk in the parish) but there had been no legally ordained minister for several years before the Revd Hugh Kemp was so appointed in May 1701.

By now many houses had timber-built second and third storeys, with heather and furze roofs, outside stone stairs which projected so far into the street that they narrowed the road for traffic, middens at the bottom and bunkers below them in which pigs, fowl and dogs were housed. The High Street had only three roads running from it – Collier Raw (Bruce Street) and Cross Wynd to the north, and Kirkgate to the south. The Tron Burn ran in front of the houses on the east of Collier Raw, along the foot of the High Street, and down under a house in the Kirkgate, reappearing in the Maygate.

The nineteenth century saw the rise of industry, here as elsewhere, with weaving, coal mining and trade predominating. The arrival of the steam loom did away with the traditional hand-loom weaving, a cottage industry, and promoted the growth of factories. It was such innovations which drove many to emigrate to the New World, among them the young Andrew Carnegie. His story is told in more detail from page 57 onwards.

Despite Dunfermline's thwarted ambitions to become the county town and its brief status as a city, it did grow in size and importance. The population rose to some 18,000 in the 1870s with 25,000 in the city and parish as a whole.

THE TWENTIETH CENTURY

The twentieth century was the time of transport and Carnegie-inspired improvements, a boom in defence work and a recession when it went away.

In 1904 the Dunfermline & District Tramways Company was formed, although trams did not run until 1909 (and continued till 1937). The network linked the town with its suburbs and the mining villages of West Fife. By 1914 there was an extensive railway system and the building of the Forth Bridge had opened up new export markets for cloth and coal. Textile manufacture relied increasingly on female labour as the powered looms in factories replaced traditional cottage industry. This also meant that women worked less in the coal mines. Instead, miners' wives and daughters came from Cowdenbeath, Lochore and other towns to work in the linen mills. The line linking Dunfermline to Rosyth – Scotland's first and only garden suburb – and the establishment of the naval dockyard increased prosperity.

Leisure also benefited. People wanted to travel to football matches at Dunfermline Athletic, Cowdenbeath and further afield; pleasure cruising on the Forth and railway excursions became more commonplace; the music halls and, later, cinema, proved strong draws; there were more civic amenities – many provided by Carnegie – such as public baths, the gymnasium, library, billiard hall, schools, institutes, hospitals and Pittencrieff Park with its tearoom, bandstand, paddling pool, zoo and gardens.

But the navy left Rosyth dockyard as the Peace Dividend and bone-headed political decisions removed its *raison d'être*. There are hopes that its fortunes can be restored (page 124) and the new ferry terminal now links Dunfermline and Rosyth with ports across the North Sea.

The shape of industry has changed too – the mainstays of the local economy are no longer weaving and mining, but software and services. The 'Auld Grey Toun' is rapidly gaining a reputation as the home of computer games. And as the new millennium provided a British parliament dominated by east coast Scots – including the local MP Gordon Brown, Chancellor of the Exchequer – and a Scottish parliament with limited but crucial powers over the economy, there is renewed hope.

Political whim can grant or take away administrative autonomy. It can remove at a stroke long-cherished titles such as city and royal burgh. It can encourage, discourage or even destroy entire industries and the communities they support. But it cannot hollow out the heart from a proud people. Today, there is no wealthy benefactor on the scale of Carnegie to endow and sustain the town so it falls to the Dunfermline folk to look after their own. But then, they have been doing so quite adequately for 1,000 years and could probably continue well enough if left alone to get on with it. Kings, palaces and parliaments come and go, as do councils and economic development quangos. People, families, neighbourhoods remain. 'Esto Rupe Inaccessa' the burgh motto says – 'This Rock Shall Not Be Surmounted'. Carry on, Dunfermline: you're doing fine.

From the Abbey to Kirkgate

The abbey in its ruined post-Reformation state is shown in this 1670 engraving by E. Henderson LLD. Alexander I made Stirling a royal burgh in 1109 and probably granted Dunfermline its burgh charter in the same year, or certainly by 1112. To further adorn the church, he erected the two massive towers at the western entrance, a west gable with a grand entrance, great west window above it and a peaked roof. *(DCL)*

Following the marriage between Malcolm Canmore and Margaret a 'great flowing-in of malcontents from England occurred', as a later chronicler put it. Although the English were found in every sizeable town and village in Scotland, Dunfermline, as the seat of royalty, would have seen the largest number. Among the consequences of this were the introduction of the arts, the growing influence of Anglo-Saxon over Gaelic (which laid the foundation of today's Lowland Scots) and the beginning of what Margaret and her retinue would regard as civilization. Dunfermline was, and remained, Scotland's metropolis until the death of King James I in 1436 over 350 years later. To reinforce its new status as the important centre of an emerging nation, it required a large church. The small, ancient Culdee church and the chapel in the Tower (if there was one) would have been neither suitable for the larger number of worshippers, nor to their taste. Around 1072 – or at least very soon after the nuptials – Margaret and Turgot put a plan for a new church to Malcolm, who agreed to it but also wanted it to outstrip every other ecclesiastical building in Scotland for size and architectural splendour. He also envisaged a place of royal sepulture – a burial ground for himself and all future kings of the Scots. So he founded the Church of the Holy Trinity and enriched it with gifts and revenues. Queen Margaret was clearly thrilled. She enriched Dunfermline Abbey with jewels of high value, intricate gold and silver vessels and a black cross with many diamonds, which she had brought from England. Initially there were at least two altars in the church: the High Altar (Grate Awtre) at the east and the Altar of the Holy Cross or Rood Altar (Rwde Awtre) to the south. Building must have started quickly for by 1075 the abbey was partially open for worship. It appears to have taken forty years to complete, but a temporary wall allowed the worshippers to use the easternmost part. The usurper Donald Bane co-occupied the throne for two periods between 1093 and 1097 in uneasy alliance with his nephew Edmund. But Malcolm's line was restored by Edgar during his short reign (1097–1107). He made little progress with the abbey building work, but gave several possessions to it to raise sufficient funds. His brother and successor, Alexander I, completed the church around 1115. It is impossible to overstate the importance of Dunfermline Abbey in the medieval period. Not only was it was one of the richest Scottish religious houses, owning almost all of West Fife as well as property in other counties, it also had civil and criminal jurisdiction equal to that of the crown. The abbey churchyard succeeded Iona as the burial place of kings and it was the Westminster Abbey of Scotland. *(DCL)*

In 1304 the monastery attached to the abbey was set ablaze by King Edward I of England, possibly in retribution for the rebellious parliaments which had been held there in William Wallace's time. In a few hours the magnificent building was in ruins. The abbey itself escaped damage. Edward may also have destroyed Malcolm Canmore's Tower (page 14), making a new royal residence necessary. The new palace was definitely completed by 1323 because the second son of Robert Bruce – later King David II – was born there. The ruins of the palace were excavated in 1923. *(MA DCL)*

King Robert I (Robert Bruce) was buried in the abbey in 1329. He died of leprosy, aged fifty-five. He had lived in Dunfermline Palace while taking the curative waters at nearby Scotlandwell where the Red Friars kept a hospital. His marble tomb was specially made in Paris. Later his heart was exhumed by his son David II to send on a crusade and was eventually enshrined at Melrose Abbey. His tomb was discovered by accident in 1808. The king now rests under the suitably ornate pulpit and the tower bears his name, carved out of the stone. *(DCL)*

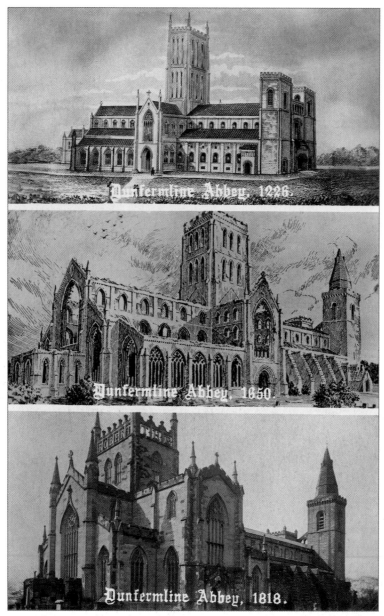

The abbey church, partially demolished during riots in 1560, seems to have been repaired in 1564, although worship continued in the ruined kirk during the intervening period. Further repairs to the nave were made in 1570. However, by 1601 the abbey was in ruins, the tops of the walls covered with grass and the nave used as a mere parish kirk by the new Protestant congregation. This was despite the work of William Schaw, architect to King James VI and a much loved and respected man, famous for his learning and his honesty. He had been charged with the restoration of the abbey in 1594 and built the steeple, some of the buttresses, the roofs of the north and south aisles, the north porch, and part of the west gable above the great door. He also planned and built Queen Anne's House and the Bailie and Constabulary Houses. Schaw's work was taken over and completed in 1607 by the newly created Earl of Dunfermline and Constable of Dunfermline Palace, Alexander Seton. Early on a Sunday morning in April 1716 the Great Lantern or Central Tower fell. Situated at the junction of the choir and the nave, it was at least 150 feet high and about 30 feet square, with two storeys of three tall Gothic lancet windows on all sides. Part of the reason for the collapse was the many deep graves dug around its foundations. The east gable of the choir fell into the kirkyard in 1726. In 1728 the roof, steeple and church bells were repaired. The inscription 'King Robert the Bruce' around the tower dates from the new construction of 1818–21, which suggests the bottom picture is dated too early. *(DCL)*

Elizabeth of Bohemia, born in Dunfermline Palace in 1596, was the daughter of James VI and Anne of Denmark. She married Frederick V of Bohemia and through her daughter Sophie, who married George I, provided the link between the Stewarts and the Hanovers. *(DCL)*

Queen Elizabeth II visited the abbey on its 900th anniversary in 1972. Here she is with Provost Crawford while the Duke of Edinburgh engages the Revd Stuart MacPherson in conversation. *(DCL)*

Abbot House in Maygate, 1908. The original hand-coloured drawing shows it was coloured a controversial pink even then. The house was built in the 1450s for Abbot Richard Bothwell and was the abbot's residence until Commendator George Durie decided to occupy more sumptuous apartments in the palace in 1540. After thirty years of neglect it again became the home of the Commendator, Robert Pitcairn, up to his death in 1584. Pitcairn added the north and south towers. It was further extended over the centuries and became a craft school and the Naturalist Society museum in the early 1900s. During the Second World War it was the Naval Officers' Club and headquarters of the Air Training Corps. After a period post-war as premises of the Naturalist Society museum again, a Dunfermline Presbytery building and a doctor's surgery, it became a Heritage Centre in the 1990s. The grounds have now been laid out as a seventeenth-century herb garden. *(DCL)*

Abbot Street before the parish council offices were built in 1912. *(DCL)*

Compare this with the picture above, taken from the same viewpoint. The parish council offices in Abbot Street had lost their original function by the late 1970s. They now house the property services department of Fife Council. *(DCL)*

James Wilson, outside his shop at 8–10 Abbot Street, *c.* 1900. He gave his name to Wilson's Close which runs up the side of the building. He could have been the model for Granpaw Broon. The shop itself can be seen towards the left-hand side of the upper picture on the previous page but not in the lower one. The site is now occupied by a hairdressing salon. *(DCL)*

Abbot House (see page 24) from the back and the abbey churchyard, *c.* 1880. Queen Margaret and her eldest son Edward were interred here, as was Malcolm Canmore eventually (1115) when his remains were brought back from Alnwick. Duncan II, Malcolm's immediate successor and his son by his first marriage to Ingibjorg, is also said to have been buried at Dunfermline after his assassination in 1095. The usurper Donald Bane co-occupied the throne for two periods between 1093 and 1097 in uneasy alliance with his nephew Edmund. Malcolm's line was restored by Edgar during his short reign (1097–1107) and by Alexander I. Both were buried here, as was their brother and successor, David I (1124–53). In 1117 Prince Ethelrede died while visiting his sister Matilda, Queen of England, and his remains were conveyed to Dunfermline for burial beside his beloved mother and his brothers. Only Canmore's traitorous son Edmund is missing – his life was spared by Edgar, but he spent his last few years exiled in a monastery and, full of remorse, requested to be buried in chains when he died around 1100. He was the last Scottish king to be buried on the isle of Iona. *(DCL)*

Kirkgate in the 1860s before the new Town House was built (see page 32). *(DCL)*

Kirkgate in the twentieth century. The Town House is apparent, as is the Victorian building beside the Abbey Tavern. *(DCL)*

This 1900 view of the Kirkgate and the back of the corporation buildings in Maygate was taken from an old lantern slide. *(DCL)*

At the beginning of the twentieth century the coach to Limekilns and Charlestown left from the Abbey Tavern in the Kirkgate. The tavern itself was owned by the same Cowan family from 1845 to 1975. The building beyond it became a nightclub and a hair studio. *(DCL)*

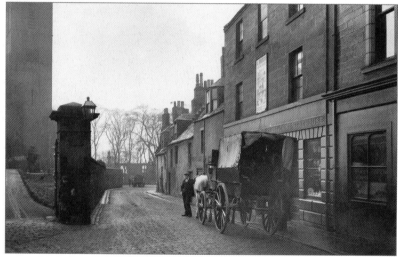

A modern picture of an old building. The Old Inn in Kirkgate was originally an eighteenth-century building, but it was reconstructed in the Victorian era. It is reputedly the oldest tavern in Dunfermline. Good pint, though. The Abbey Tavern next door is now the Creepy Wee Pub. *(DCL)*

Goodall's horse-bus, with Mr Finlayson driving as usual, took these trippers as far afield as the Tormaukin Hotel in Glen Devon at the heady pace of 7 miles per hour. It is unclear from the photograph whether the passengers are anxious to get into the hostelry, or unsteady after their sojourn there. Goodall's carriages were based in Queen Anne Street. The building later became Goodall's garage and was demolished in 1981. *(DCL)*

Fraser & Carmichael's warehouse in Kirkgate in 1970, just before the firm closed for good. Established in 1866 Fraser & Co. eventually had a number of shops in the area and also owned the City Hotel and McLay's Brewery in Alloa. At the peak of the mining activity before 1914 it was selling over a ton of tallow every week to miners for their lamps. The building shown was demolished in 1973 and the site is now a green space. *(DCL)*

The first recorded election of magistrates and council occurred in 1488. The old council had met in the Praetoria or Tollbooth. As well as a provost, bailies and serjeants, fourteen councillors are named and various of them received the no doubt lucrative duties of flesh pricers, *liniatores* (inspectors of weights and measures), birlawmen (assessors of fines) and *gustatores cervisiae* (ale-tasters, probably a sought-after position). Councillors, when elected, processed down Kirkgate to the abbey for the kirkin' of the council, a ceremony lost since the autonomy of Dunfermline was removed although it continued in a different guise, and not always in Dunfermline, under the District Council until 1995. This picture shows the ceremony in 1972. *(DCL)*

A Walk up the High Street

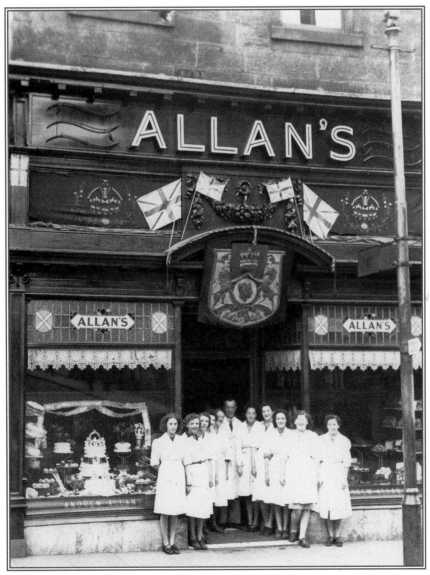

Allan's bakery in the High Street – here decked out *c.* 1950 – eventually became McVities Guest. *(DCL)*

Above: Work started on the new Town House in 1876. Under the foundation stone was laid a time capsule with money and newspapers of the day, and an artist's impression of the finished structure. This building replaced the 1771 Town House which in turn had supplanted the building removed when Bridge Street was built. It is typical of Scottish Baronial-style civic buildings that sprang up all over the country at the end of the Victorian era. The spire was added to allow the four faces of the clock to be seen from all parts of the town. The ground floor was initially a bank branch office, but the whole building became the Council Chambers in 1879. *(DCL)*

The Town House was open by 1880 when this photograph was taken. But what was everyone doing there at 7.34 in the morning? Notice also that the Glen Gates (see page 73) had not yet been constructed. They would not be built for another forty-seven years. *(DCL)*

The High Street saw its share of parades, like the 1899 Barnum and Bailey circus visit. No elephants are in evidence in the picture, but the exotic apparel of the horses and performers no doubt made up for it. *(DCL)*

There's nothing like a decent accident to get the crowds out. This girder was destined for a bridge in Cairneyhill in 1904 but ended up outside No. 7 High Street instead. *(DCL)*

By 1917, when this photograph was taken, the trams had been running for eight years. Trams ran from the depot in St Leonard's Street to Townhill, Rosyth and Rumblingwell, and further afield to Lochore and Kelty. This one bears an advert for Dick's Cooperative Institutions (see page 47). We can only presume the dog moved in good time. *(DCL)*

The Wee Sweetie Shop was a well-known fixture in the High Street in the years after the First World War. *(DCL)*

The High Street was originally Hie Gait and Causeygate – the only street in the medieval town with a causeway stone surface. Not only did it have many small closes running off it north and south, many of which still survived in 1922 when this photograph was taken, it was also the site of the market. Dunfermline had no Market Square as such. Notice the electric street lighting and the tram intersection. *(MA DCL)*

The High Street at the turn of the twentieth century. Lipton's (see over page) is on the left, with Drysdale's drapery and outfitters and Tyler's shoe shop on the right. This photograph shows the number of message boys who were employed in the retail trade in the days before motorized transport or trams. *(DCL)*

Above: Inside Thomas Lipton's in the 1920s was an impressive array of foodstuffs in addition to the famous tea. The self-styled 'king of the dairy trade' opened his first Lipton Market in Anderston, Glasgow, in 1871, selling not only butter, eggs and ham (his Irish roots showing through), but also own-brand tea and coffee grown in his own Ceylon plantations. Sugar at 3lb for 2*d* is one eightieth of the price in 2002. Lipton also pioneered pictorial advertising and shop window displays, such as his famous 'wooden ham'. *(DCL)*

Where would we be without Woolie's? The first Dunfermline shop opened in 1922 and translated the American 'five and dime' concept into 'Everything 3*d* or 6*d*'. The threepenny Easter eggs in the window and the sixpenny skipping rope are examples. The shop was infested with rats and the manager, Mr Smith, had a mongoose to keep them down. The building is now an electrical store and the attic gable has disappeared. Woolworth's later moved across the street. *(DCL)*

Boots also appeared in Dunfermline in the 1920s but is shown here in the early 1930s. The site at 63–65 High Street now has a more modern and longer frontage. *(DCL)*

Below: In 1939 war was imminent. In Dunfermline High Street, buses had replaced trams (in 1937), cars were no longer a novelty and everybody wore a hat – probably bought at Hepworth's on the corner of Guildhall Street where a building society now stands. The Bruce Café is now part of Boots. Woolworth's, seen on the right and level with the bus, is now Poundstretcher. *(DCL)*

For anyone who has ever wondered what a bank safe looks like, there was ample opportunity to see this one being installed in the High Street branch of the Royal Bank in 1956. Two-way car traffic had only recently stopped and pedestrianization was thirty years away. *(MA DCL)*

The Royal Bank building succumbed to the consumerism of the 1990s and became a McDonald's – although there is a certain piquancy to burgers being served up in a listed building. *(DCL)*

Thomson the watchmaker, having a clearance sale before a facelift . . . *(DCL)*

. . . and after. *(DCL)*

By 1976 many of the famous businesses in the High Street and East Port had closed or were looking decidedly dowdy. Even Thomson's (see previous page) had disappeared. The Regal was later acquired by Littlewoods but suffered vandalism and a fire. *(DCL)*

The 1990s witnessed the height of ill-feeling against the Poll Tax, a fiscal disaster which was abandoned in 1993 and led to the downfall of Conservative Prime Minister Margaret Thatcher. The then government created a rod for its own back by imposing the tax first on Scotland with its higher proportion of council tenants and traditional leftist persuasion. The Scots were naturally rebellious against the 'Tory Tax', devising measures to defeat sheriffs, bailiffs and court cases. *(DCL)*

The look of the High Street had changed by the 1990s with many well-known local shops disappearing to be replaced by chain multiples and ground-floor façades swapped for plate glass. Various attempts at pedestrianization by stealth – trial schemes, closure for water mains renewals, etc. – culminated in the 'New Look' High Street in about 1992. *(DCL)*

During the 1990s many famous shops disappeared, including the Co-op in the High Street, which had occupied this and nearby buildings since the 1860s. Partial pedestrianization had also allowed the emergence of 'street furniture'. This building is possibly due for demolition. *(DCL)*

There is definitely a message here – a building that starts out in 1809 as a linen exchange and Guildhall for the prosperous burghers and merchants of the town, becomes a pub from 1817 until 1845, a police station and county court from about 1850, and ends the next century as a JobCentre. There were hopes that it would be the county chambers if Dunfermline became county town in the mid-nineteenth century, but that honour went to Cupar instead. The spire was added by public subscription in 1811. *(DCL)*

This once-famous picture, now seldom seen in print, depicts Daft Archie, a Dunfermline worthy, born in 1801. Archie was the subject of much torment from the schoolboys of Dunfermline, who used to entice him to open his large mouth so they could pitch pennies into it. He died aged seventy-six, so his itinerant ways must have sustained him. The shop behind him is Beveridge the tobacconist, now the site of Burton's. The original picture, painted by A. Geddes in 1903, hangs in the City Chambers. *(DCL)*

From Bridge Street to Pilmuir

This photograph of Bruce Street must date from before 1925 as the Caledonia Works in Damside Street burned down that year. *(DCL)*

In 1496 'the communitie of Dunfermlyn has consentit til open the burn at the west gavil of the tolbuith'. Later known as the Back Burn, it runs south under Bridge Street. This is Bridge Street some time before 1928. The commercial traveller with his hampers of goods is outside Fairfield's. Opposite are Anderson's drapery (later Bruce & Glen, grocers), MacPherson's bookshop (on the site of Craig's brewery, later at Regal Close and now Chalmers Street) and the ironmongers, Coull & Matthew. *(DCL)*

Before the Glen Bridge opened in 1932, Bruce Street looked like this. The shops continue into Damside Street and Sclar's furniture shop is on the right. *(DCL)*

The construction of the Glen Bridge from the Chalmers Street end, 1931. The wooden frame supported the poured concrete. The bridge crosses the gorge cut by the Tower Burn joining Carnegie Drive to Pittencrieff Street. Though it only took some eighteen months to complete, the idea had taken 120 years to come to fruition after the first proposal in 1810. *(DCL)*

The elegant Grade B-listed Glen Bridge was completed in 1932 at a cost of some £40,000. It was an early example of a substantial open-spandrel reinforced concrete structure. It received major (and award-winning) restoration and upgrading in 1992 to cope with increased traffic. The work cost over £1 million. *(DCL)*

Bruce Street after the Glen Bridge was built. McKenzie the draper and Lessell's wine merchant (later Anderson's) are on the left. *(DCL)*

The old Pittencrieff Street is mostly gone. The part from Coal Road to Urquart Road was known as James Place. It has been replaced by newer houses and empty ground. *(DCL)*

DCI – Dick's Co-operative Institutions – was a local legend. Starting with a small shop in 1886 it grew to have many branches, including this butchery at 61 Queen Anne Street. The firm closed down in 1956. *(DCL)*

Dick's didn't have things all their own way. The Co-op butchers were just as well respected. This is the Randolph Street shop in 1913. *(DCL)*

The Opera House in Reform Street never staged an opera. Farces, musical comedies and stars like Will Fyfe and Harry Lauder (see page 86) appeared in the 1930s, as well as 'straight' stage plays. The size of the audiences is a testament to its popularity in the days before television. Some of the interiors were salvaged and incorporated in the Asola Theatre, Sarasota, Florida, which was based on the Opera House design. The Opera House caught fire on 15 May 1982. *(DCL)*

Dunfermline Post Office, seen from Pilmuir Street, 1956. Originally the post office was in two rooms in a Maygate building, but moved in 1852 to the top of Guildhall Street and again twenty years later to the High Street. These purpose-built premises at Pilmuir Street and Queen Anne Street were opened in 1890. They were later extended on to ground owned by the adjacent Dunfermline High School – where the Grammar School had stood until the 1624 fire. The proceeds from the sale of the land were used to build a new school in Priory Lane. *(DCL)*

Below: Bath Street became Pilmuir Street after this 1915 photograph was taken. *(DCL)*

Music hall gave way to cinema eventually. The Palace Kinema in Pilmuir Street, seen here in the 1930s, advertised a 'Rich' programme – the manager Mr J. Rich evidently had a sense of humour. He always wore evening dress to add a touch of class. *(DCL)*

Below: Pilmuir Works, 1997. This Grade A-listed building is at the junction of Pilmuir Street and Foundry Street. Built in 1849 as an extension to the first power loom factory in the town, it had elevations added between 1888 and 1901. In 1926 it was taken over by Hay & Robertson and a bridge – known as the Bridge of Sighs – was built to link it with St Margaret's Works across Foundry Street. In 1939 plans to demolish it in favour of a trading estate were halted and it was used as a hostel for Rosyth dockyard workers. In 1947 the works became the home of Dunlop textiles, weaving fabric for tyres. *(DCL)*

The intersection of Arthur Street and Pilmuir Street was a quieter place (above) before the building of the Broomhead Drive flats in the 1960s (left). *(DCL)*

Campbell Street, *c.* 1935. The corner shop was still there. Someone has hung an improving message from an upstairs window. The street corner retains an odour of sanctity – a religious meeting house now stands in the shop's place. *(DCL)*

In 1981 Campbell was still selling motor bikes and scooters in the Campbell Street premises. The building is now a Bargain Centre, although bike sales continue next door. *(DCL)*

Elder's City Mills in Campbell Street were built in 1908. The mills shut in the 1970s. Elder's house, Pitbauchlie, became a hotel. *(DCL)*

Elder's works milled grain. However, the company had started life as grain merchants and only began milling oatmeal in 1905. During the Second World War the plant worked day and night to produce over 5,000 tons of meal a year, a lot of it intended for the forces overseas. *(DCL)*

The old Campbell Street fire station went out of use in 1936 when the new one was built in Carnegie Drive. It is said that the council bought a new fire engine that year, only to find that it wouldn't go into the building with the ladder on. It had to be removed each time the engine returned to the station and refitted if there was a call-out – not exactly conducive to rapid response. (DCL)

The new fire station opened in April 1936. Despite plans for a newer station in the 1980s, and pressure from local businesses, it remains stubbornly in place. The style is modernist but not far removed from the Art Deco example in nearby Kirkcaldy. (DCL)

Carnegie Street, 1960. This view has changed out of all recognition today; it has been supplanted by the dual carriageway of Carnegie Drive, the Kingsgate shopping centre (page 116), the bus station and other changes. *(DCL)*

Carnegie Drive is also the site of the new bus station. It was constructed between 1979 and 1984. *(DCL)*

The Carnegie Legacy and Pittencrieff Park

Richard Goulden's statue of Andrew Carnegie was erected in 1914, suitably
elevating the great benefactor. *(DCL)*

'This, then, is held to be the duty of the man of wealth: first, to set an example of modest unostentatious living, shunning display; to provide moderately for the legitimate wants of those dependent upon him; and, after doing so, to consider all surplus revenues which come to him simply as trust funds which he is strictly bound as a matter of duty to administer in the manner which, in his judgement, is best calculated to produce the most beneficial results for the community.'

Andrew Carnegie, *The Gospel of Wealth*, 1889
(Note that by the next year, Carnegie's annual income was $25 million).

As everyone surely knows, the American iron and steel magnate and philanthropist Andrew Carnegie (1835–1919) was born in Dunfermline. His father, a cottage weaver, emigrated to the USA in 1848 and the thirteen-year-old Andrew began work almost immediately as a threading machine attendant in a cotton mill in Allegheny, Pennsylvania, paid $1.20 a week. He later took a job in a factory tending the steam engine and boiler, for $2.00 per week. He impressed his supervisor with his penmanship and was offered the chance to work as a clerk. In 1849 he became a messenger in a Pittsburgh telegraph office. He memorized the names of people to whom he had taken messages and was able to save time by recognizing them on the street. Soon after he was promoted to the position of telegraph operator at the princely salary of $20 per month. In 1853 he joined the Pennsylvania Railroad as the personal telegrapher and assistant to Thomas Alexander Scott, superintendent of the railroad's western division, and was paid $35 per month. Carnegie was consistently promoted until he became superintendent of the Pittsburgh part of the railroad, and was responsible for innovations such as keeping the telegraph office open twenty-four hours a day and burning railroad cars after accidents, which cleared the tracks and got the trains moving quickly. Ever thrifty, he borrowed from a local bank and invested $217.50 in the Woodruff Sleeping Car Company (later the Pullman Company). Within two years he was receiving an annual dividend of about $5,000, more than three times his railroad salary.

During the Civil War Scott was in charge of military transportation and government telegraphs for the Union Army. Carnegie served under him, supervising repairs to the railroad and telegraph lines damaged by the Confederacy. Having seen the potential of both steel and steam, after the war Carnegie formed a company to make iron railroad bridges and a steel mill, one of the first to use the new Bessemer process. He invested his returns from the sleeping car business – some $11,000 – in an oil company in Titusville, Pennsylvania, and received a return of $17,868 after only one year. At the age of thirty-three he had an annual income of $50,000. He said at the time: 'Beyond this, never earn, make no effort to increase fortune, but spend the surplus each year for benevolent purposes.'

In 1868 he determined to retire from business, aged thirty-five, but it wasn't to be. Two years later he met Louise Whitfield, the daughter of a wealthy merchant; she was later to become his wife. In 1872 on a visit to Britain Carnegie visited Henry Bessemer's steel plants. The Freedom Iron Company, which Carnegie had formed in 1861, had been using Bessemer's process for several years, but Carnegie now realized the greater commercial potential of steel and returned to America with plans to expand his business. However, he did donate the first Carnegie Baths to Dunfermline the next year, 1873.

It wasn't until 1887, and his mother's death, that Carnegie married Louise. Ten years later their daughter Margaret was born. Louise urged Andrew to buy a home in Scotland. All he required was that it should have a view of the sea, a waterfall and a trout stream. He settled for Skibo Castle in Dornoch, which was in ruins and had no waterfall, paying £85,000. (Skibo is from the Celtic *schytherbolle*, meaning 'fairyland' or 'place of peace'.) Louise supervised the reconstruction, and Andrew got his waterfall in the garden: he could see and hear it from his study.

In 1899 he rationalized all his interests in the Carnegie Steel Company, which then accounted for almost a quarter of all American iron and steel production. As he said to Mark Twain: 'Put all your eggs in one basket and then watch that basket.' In 1901 he sold out to his main competitor, J.P. Morgan's United States Steel Corporation, for $250 million, becoming possibly the world's richest man – his total net worth was the equivalent of more than $100 billion in 2001, twice what Microsoft's Bill Gates had that year. Then he finally retired to devote himself to good works.

The weaver's cottage in Moodie Street, between the butcher's and the fix-it shop, where Andrew Carnegie was born in 1835 and brought up prior to the family's emigration. Many of the houses in this street were occupied by hand-loom weavers. The street was built in 1781 and named in 1809 after a recent ex-provost. Now a museum, the cottage is the only such building in the street. It has a working Jacquard hand-loom, similar to that used by Andrew's father William, which clacks into action on the first Friday of each month during the tourist season. *(DCL)*

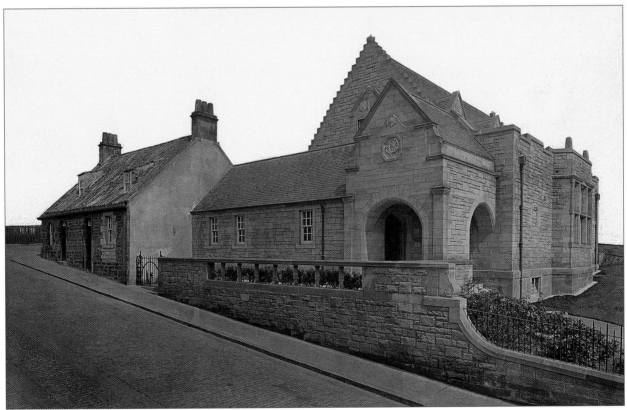

The Carnegie Memorial was later added to the humble cottage. It was endowed by Mrs Louise Carnegie to document and display the meteoric business career of her husband from bobbin boy, telegraph operator and railroad developer to steel king of America. *(DCL)*

But his charitable activities had already started. His first gift was in 1873 and his largest was in 1911 for $125 million to the Carnegie Corporation of New York. He also donated money for the construction of what is now the International Court of Justice for the United Nations at The Hague, The Netherlands. Because Carnegie had never received a formal education, but had been inspired by his self-taught uncle George Lauder (page 76), and his mother's Chartist relatives, he donated more then $350 million to educational, cultural, and peace organizations. He endowed hundreds of libraries worldwide – he had been deeply affected by being refused free membership in Colonel James Anderson's Mechanics' and Apprentices' Library in Allegheny City in 1853 – and above the doors of The Carnegie Library of Pittsburgh are his own words: 'Free to the People'. Carnegie also paid for 10,000 church organs. At his death his last $30 million was given away to charities, foundations and pensioners.

Carnegie gave a fair proportion of his fortune to the benefit of Scotland in general and Dunfermline in particular. 'It is the mind that makes the body rich,' he said. 'There is no class so pitiably wretched as that which possesses money and nothing else.'

Carnegie, though a giant of industry, was small of stature – somewhere around 5 feet 4 inches – but he was determined, disciplined and tough. However, he could also be naïve. He promoted both the rights of workers to organize into unions and the employer's right to break strikes with violence if necessary. He tried to buy independence for the Philippines, regarding their purchase by America from Spain as imperialistic, yet his rather touching support of the German kaiser, in an apparent belief that he was promoting world peace, earned him a fair degree of criticism in his last years. He remained optimistic about human nature and had an enduring faith in the common sense and nobility of the human spirit. The First World War – most definitely a war of steel – must have saddened him. He left Scotland for the last time in 1914 to settle at Shadowbrook, Massachusetts, where he died on 11 August 1919 aged eighty-five.

Carnegie wasn't always popular. The *Dunfermline Press* lampooned him for his support of the kaiser when feelings were running high at the start of the First World War. *(DPG)*

Above: Andrew Carnegie's mother Margaret laid the memorial stone for the world's first Carnegie Library on Wednesday 27 July 1881 and the council declared a half-day holiday. The library was opened in 1883, as this clipping shows, by the Earl of Rosebery. *(DCL/DPG)*

The world's first Carnegie Library in Abbot Street, 1906. The building is substantially the same today, despite the fire in 1961, but an extension was added down St Margaret Street in 1992. *(DCL)*

The Carnegie Trust was keen to encourage all sorts of educational activities among the children of Dunfermline. This 1906 photograph shows the first children's flower show in the Bruce Street Drill Hall. The gentleman in the tile hat is Dr MacDonald, Rector of the High School, alongside Sir John Ross, then chairman of the Carnegie Dunfermline Trust. *(DCL)*

The crowds in Bonnar Street waiting for a glimpse of Carnegie and his wife on their way to lay the memorial stone of the baths and gymnasium on 16 July 1902. The procession was led by pipers from the Dunfermline Volunteer Company. *(DCL)*

The original baths, founded by Carnegie's gift in 1873, opened in 1877. They had somewhat limited facilities, notably lack of spectator seating, so Carnegie offered a further £20,000 in 1900 for new baths and a gymnasium. The Carnegie Central Baths opened in 1905 and the building is now the Carnegie Centre. *(DCL)*

The original Carnegie Baths at the corner of Pilmuir Street, shown here and in the picture above, were last used as such in 1926 and closed in 1927. Mixed bathing? For shame, Mr Langston and Mr Martin. But who's the lady? *(DCL)*

The Carnegie Baths were being demolished when this photograph was taken in 1971. They had ceased being baths in 1927 and became the Pilmur Hall and later offices for the Department of Social Security. When the Carnegie Dunfermline Trust planned the new Carnegie Centre in 1899 – as a replacement for the original 1870s Carnegie Baths – they reinforced the aims of 'Purity in Youth, Strength in Manhood'. The building was closed for almost three years from 1979 for improvements, which continued in three phases. Now the centre boasts better pools, a fitness centre, sports hall and other amenities. *(DCL/DPG)*

Interior of Turkish Baths, Dunfermline.

The Turkish baths were an exotic addition to the Carnegie edifice. It is an interesting sidelight to Carnegie's legacy that the Usher Vaux Championships were abolished in 1967 because swimming was so strong in the town that no other team could compete with the Carnegie club. *(DCL)*

Carnegie Baths also housed a dental clinic, shown here in the 1930s, and other health facilities (below). *(DCL)*

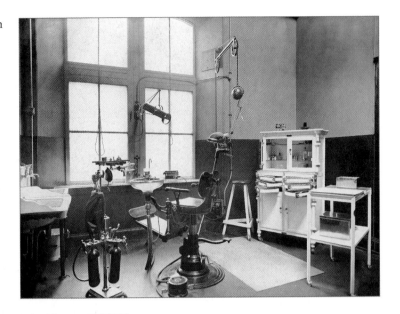

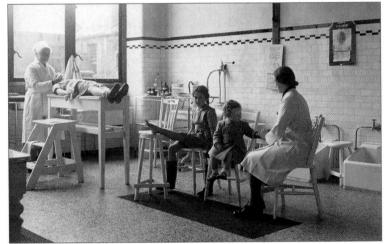

Above and right: The orthopaedic clinic at the Carnegie Baths – respiratory exercises and standing up straight lessons – was a model for similar institutions world wide. *(DCL)*

The Carnegie Clinic building in Inglis Street was constructed between 1909 and 1912 and is now one of Dunfermline's many Grade A-listed structures. The clinic was also the home of the College of Hygiene and Physical Education (see below). From 1939 to 1945 it served as a hospital for wounded soldiers and the college element was transferred to Aberdeen, out of harm's way. Afterwards the child welfare, dental and sunlight clinics continued to operate. *(DCL)*

The Carnegie Dunfermline College of Hygiene and Physical Training – the famous 'Dumf' – opened in October 1905. It was founded by the Carnegie Trust as a training college for women. Initially only a small gymnasium in Canmore Street Baths, in 1908 it was opened to men and in 1909 was taken over by the Scottish Education Department as a central institution. In 1913–14 new buildings were erected and responsibility for training was assumed by the National Committee for the Training of Teachers in 1921. From 1931 it became all-female again – male students were transferred to Jordanhill College, Glasgow. The buildings were commandeered by the navy during the Second World War, and in 1966 the college transferred to its current campus in Cramond, Edinburgh. As part of Moray House College of Education it admitted male students again in the 1980s and became the Scottish Centre for Physical Education, Movement and Leisure Studies. Now it is part of Edinburgh University and has no connection with either Dunfermline or the Carnegie Trust. And they probably don't have a regulation hairstyle any more. *(DCL)*

'How do you get to Carnegie Hall?' 'Practise!' The Carnegie Hall complex, seen here from Holyrood Place, was built between 1933 and 1937. It began life as Hawthorne Bank, became Benachie House in 1909, and was bought and converted into a music institute in 1933. During the Second World War it was a YMCA Centre for the services (page 101). The adjacent site was chosen for the erection of a concert hall after years of wrangling. The West Window is particularly interesting: it was commissioned by Andrew Carnegie from Tiffany's of New York as a memorial window for the abbey but was rejected by the Commissioners for Historic Buildings and ended up here. *(DCL)*

Pittencrieff Park – or Dunfermline Glen, as it is also known – became a mecca for pleasure seekers and day trippers as soon as it opened. The story goes that Andrew Carnegie had sneaked in as a boy to enjoy the quiet pleasures of what was then a country estate. When rich, he determined that everyone should have the same pleasure and purchased it in 1902, gifting it to the town the next year. Patrick Geddes, among others, was drafted in to develop it – somewhat overambitiously. In 1907 the Botanic Garden in Washington DC donated over 150 exotic plants. This picture was taken in the early 1900s. *(DCL)*

The famous Pittencrieff peacocks show how tame they are on the Double Bridge. It is not clear how many there are or when they were first introduced, but they have always been popular – although they have occasionally had to be culled because of the havoc they wreak on young plants. They can sometimes be seen strutting around the nearby streets and nobody pays a blind bit of notice. *(DCL)*

The Glen Falls in Pittencrieff Park and the *lin* or pool of the Ferm burn which gives Dunfermline its name. *(DCL)*

Pittencrieff Park conservatories and formal gardens, 1914. The park was laid out by James Whitton, Superintendent of Glasgow Botanic Gardens. *(DCL)*

The Pittencrieff Park bandstand, 1924.
Erected in 1909, it was built to replace
a temporary structure constructed five
years previously. It lasted until 1934
when a new version was built
adjoining the Teahouse. *(DCL)*

The Glen Gates were constructed in honour of Mrs Louise Whitfield Carnegie in 1927. She deserved them. Although Andrew idolized his mother Margaret Morrison, she effectively blocked her son's marriage until her death. Louise later said her mother-in-law was one of the most unpleasant women she had ever known. During construction of the gates a mineshaft was found, presumably sunk by the monks digging coal on the estate. The gates were spared when iron railings everywhere were being torn down for the war effort in the 1940s. *(DCL)*

The paddling pool was also a great draw. Behind is Pittencrieff House which was erected in 1610 by Sir Alexander Clerk of Penicuik. Above the door are his arms, initials and motto, 'Praised be God for all his giftes'. Over one of the windows is the crest of the Earl of Dunfermline whose estate Pittencrieff once was. It was heightened in 1731 and a third storey was added in 1740, using stones from the palace ruins. The house was bought by Andrew Carnegie, who initially intended to occupy it but never did. He gifted it to the people of Dunfermline and it is now Grade A-listed. *(DCL)*

The Pittencrieff Park Pavilion and Teahouse were still popular for outings as late as 1957. The author, then aged three, is somewhere in the front row, enthralled by the African marching band. *(DCL)*

A sight no-one will ever see again, sadly, is the cherub statue in the Lily Pond, stolen in May 1994. *(DCL)*

New Row to Nethertown

The Thomson family house in Nethertown retained the outside-stair configuration typical of the area, even after the concrete extension was added. *(DCL)*

Lauder Technical School opened in Priory Lane, next to the old Dunfermline High School, on 10 October 1899. Funded by Andrew Carnegie to the tune of £13,000, it was named after his uncle George Lauder, a long-time advocate of free technical education. Lauder had been a snuff miller, a weaver and then a blacksmith. His devotion to his children's education after the death of his wife, and to social progress in general, directly inspired Carnegie in his later charity works. It was George Lauder who provided, informally, the education the young Carnegie never got in his scant five years of schooling. Lauder died in 1901 at the age of eighty-seven, but saw his vision working – the high school and 'the tech' co-operated closely in co-educating pupils. By 1907 the 'Grey Tech' was outgrowing its premises so Andrew Carnegie offered £3,300 to supplement £5,300 from the Scottish Education Department and £3,400 from the local council to build the textile school, or 'Red Tech' as it became known, in New Row. It is pictured here soon after its opening in 1910. The 'Red Tech' is now modern flats, which incorporate part of the original sandstone façade. *(DCL)*

In 1927 the Textile School (the 'Red Tech') was merged with the Lauder Technical School (the 'Grey Tech') under Andrew Greary, who was Headmaster of the combined school for the next twenty-eight years, seeing it transformed into Lauder Technical College in 1951. In 1967 it merged with Cowdenbeath Technical College; three years later Fife Education Committee built a new college on Halbeath Road, near Fod House, and the Fife Pre-Nursing College was later incorporated. This allowed Lauder's disparate activities, spread over six or seven buildings in Dunfermline, to be brought together under one roof. This 1970 photograph shows the building just prior to opening. *(DCL/DPG)*

New Row, 1972. Traffic congestion was now becoming a major problem, as the driver of this jack-knifed lorry found to his cost. *(DCL)*

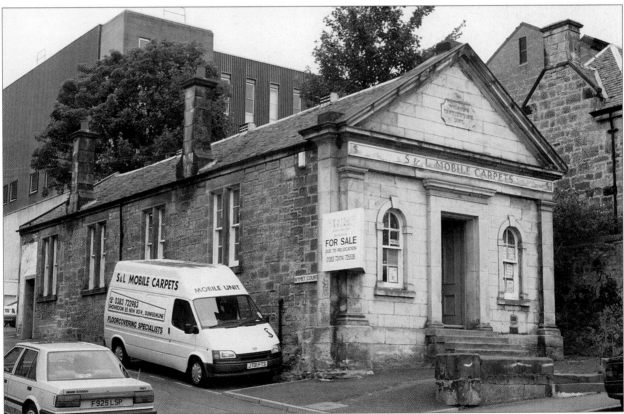

Wilson's Institute in New Row, 1996. Built in 1857, it eventually became a carpet warehouse. In September 1953 Lauder College opened a bakery in the institute. Before this, local bakers had allowed the training of apprentices to take place on their premises. The new bakery provided a dedicated training environment for bread-making, cake decoration, flour confectionery and cookery classes. *(DCL/Photograph by M. Rogers)*

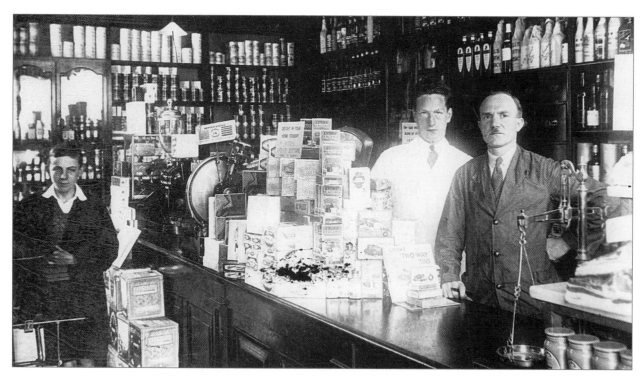

Fraser & Carmichael's shop at the corner of Canmore Street and New Row, *c*. 1935. Between the rather austere-looking manager, Mr Weir, and Willie the message boy is Alastair Dickson, father of local chanteuse Barbara Dickson. *(DCL)*

By the 1950s Whitehead's on the corner of Canmore Street and New Row had diversified into radios and electrical items. *(DCL)*

Where Moodie Street meets Nethertown Broad Street there was a typical corner shop – in this case Sharp's – selling newspapers, cigarettes and basic groceries. Most of these shops have been swept away by the appearance of the large superstores. *(DCL)*

This looks calm and peaceful, but where New Row meets Bothwell Street, Queen Margaret Drive and Nethertown Broad Street (left) there is a busy, complex junction today. The picture below shows the same area in 1957 or 1958, before the new road layout. *(left DCL; below MA DCL)*

Laying the tram lines in Canmore Street, *c.* 1909. This was originally the 'Foul Vennel' or filthy lane, and later 'In-Below-Th'-Wa's' because it followed the north boundary wall of the abbey from the eastern end of the Maygate to New Row. *(DPG)*

The elegant houses in tree-lined Park Avenue are captured on this early postcard. Even the message boy stood still for the photograph. *(DCL)*

Priory Lane bowling club and pavilion. *(DCL)*

This building in Nethertown Broad Street was the original site of the Tradesmen's Library. This 1902 drawing taken from a lantern slide shows the outside stairs typical of the period. *(DCL)*

81

Botany Bay House, 1918. It was replaced by the Nethertown Institute. Note that as well as the crow-step tiled roofs there was still some thatch in evidence on the building to the left. *(DCL)*

The Nethertown Institute, *c.* 1950. This is now the Del Farquarson Centre, named in honour of a late councillor. Institutes were founded as a way of providing recreation facilities more wholesome than pubs, gambling dens and other low places. They typically housed reading rooms, baths, a ladies' room, children's playground, billiards room and other recreational facilities. *(DCL)*

Weaving, Coal and Other Industries

In 1838 there were around 3,000 hand-looms in Dunfermline, mostly producing 'harness' work such as damask napkins and table-cloths. In 1847 steam-powered looms were introduced. Hundreds of hand-loom workers became unemployed, including Andrew Carnegie's father, Will. He may have used a loom like this in his cottage. *(DCL)*

The Pends, *c.* 1900. Between their roles as royal residence and stately ruin, these buildings served a useful purpose in the weaving industry. Weaving has been carried on in Dunfermline for centuries, but as early as 1715 a new technique called damask was in operation at Drumsheugh, near Edinburgh. For many years the process was kept secret and no-one but trusted men were even allowed to see the looms. But James Blake, a young, ingenious weaver from Dunfermline, cracked the code. Pretending to be of feeble intellect, he inveigled the Drumsheugh weavers to let him into their factory by telling them queer stories. In fact, far from being addle-brained, he was a skilled mathematician and mechanic and had a retentive memory. He memorized all the details, came back to Dunfermline, and designed a loom which he then had made by a wright and a smith. He petitioned the council to let him erect it in a room in the Pends and started damask weaving in the summer of 1718. Shortly afterwards John Beveridge and John Gilmour, weavers of Brucefield, joined Blake and filled the whole of the Pends with damask looms. Blake died 'rich, respected and regretted by the haill burgh' in about 1770 aged eighty. *(DCL)*

Dunfermline's reliance on the weaving industry is clear from the preponderance of factories – the Castleblair silk works, St Margaret's linen damask factory and the Canmore silk works at the rear of the fire station. *(DCL)*

The silk weaving industry was established with the help of key workers brought over from Switzerland. The original Castleblair Works (not a silk-weaving business) had closed in 1924. It was taken over by Gressner & Company which brought its staff in for a year to teach local workers. This 1926 photograph shows a group of Swiss, of whom the statutory 25 per cent are smiling. *(DCL)*

Hay & Robertson's linen factory, 1927. The company was a major employer of women and girls, as were the other textile businesses. *(DCL)*

The extent of the textile mills can be seen in this photograph. *(DCL)*

When Sir Harry Lauder was appearing for a week at the Opera House in March 1934, he also visited local factories, including the famous Dunfermline Silk Mills, and wowed the workers, especially the rather star-struck girl glued to his arm. Provost McKay, looking on, has obviously already had the free scarf. *(DCL)*

Coal has a long history in Dunfermline. The monks originally dug the 'black diamonds'. William of Oberville, of Pittencrieff, granted a coal charter to the abbey in 1291. In 1390 Bruce Street was known as the 'Colzier-rawe' (Collier Row). The 'Bawdrig Coal Pitts' are mentioned in a deed of 1646, coal being 'thair wrocht for hame use an for exportin'. By 1670 it was established that the profits from coal mining would be split between the town and the earls of Dunfermline and Tweeddale. Colliers' wages were between 6 and 10s a day. These would be 'shillings Scots', and as a pound Scots was worth one eighth of a pound sterling, this equates to about one English shilling, or 5p in today's currency. *(DCL)*

For years the Halkets of Pitfirrane had a government privilege of exporting coals abroad free of duty. This was renewed by Queen Anne on 21 December 1706 and ratified in the United Parliament in London in 1707 just as the Act of Union was passed. Sir Peter Halket (who, as Sir Peter Wedderburn, had married the daughter of the ex-provost Sir James Halket and changed his name in order to acquire the baronetcy and become provost in James's stead) was Dunfermline's Commissioner to the Scottish Parliament. He had been charged to vote against the Union, but merely delivered the burgh council's address to parliament and voted for it. It is hard to avoid the conclusion that he was bought off. He is said not to have shown his face in Dunfermline for a whole year, but surprisingly was subsequently re-elected provost twenty-seven times. These coal miners look less than jovial after a hard shift. They supplied their own tallow for the lamps they are carrying. *(DCL)*

Above: Women still worked in the pits in the 1920s – not down the shafts but as coal pickers and washers on the surface. This 1927 group shows how clean they were compared with their lads. *(DCL)*

Coal merchant Robert Duncan had his yard in James Street. His daughter is holding the reins of a beautifully bedecked horse some time around 1930. *(DCL)*

Above: Coal was transported from the deep faces to the hutches (wagons) by conveyer belt. This picture was taken in the Aitken Pit, Kelty. *(DCL)*

Above ground at the Aitken Pit, wagons of the Fife Coal Company were loaded for transport away. *(DCL)*

Those who yearn nostalgically for the good old days when King Coal was a major employer tend to forget the cost in human suffering from disease and disasters. Ten men died in the 1939 Valleyfield disaster. All were buried at Culross New Cemetery. *(DCL)*

Valleyfield continued in business and miners continued to work. This photograph shows the transporter at No. 1 shaft in 1955. *(DCL)*

Is my man in that? Waiting for news after the explosion at the Lindsay Pit, Kelty, in December 1957. *(MA DCL)*

The Mary Pit at Lochore had a 150-foot chimney, seen here being demolished in 1958. *(DCL)*

Longannet was the last vestige of deep coal mining at the end of the twentieth century but closed in early 2002 after it was flooded with 17 million gallons of water. Over 500 jobs were lost. This 1970s photograph shows the transfer bunkers taking coal to the adjacent power station. *(DCL)*

Opencast mining is controversial to this day, with great concerns over environmental spoiling and destruction of the landscape. Bulldozers and earthmovers scrape away the soil and rocks covering the coal deposits. This 'overburden' is used to create 'bunds' or mounds around the site. Explosives break up the coal mass and large power shovels scoop it into wagons and trucks for delivery to a processing plant. An opencast mine is generally obvious for miles around by the coal dirt left on the roads. Economics dictate that today most of the world's coal comes from opencast mines. The largest ones can spread over several square kilometres and may be more than 150 metres deep. *(DCL)*

In 1701 the population of the burgh was estimated at 2,000 and the burgh and parish at about 5,000. Trades were depressed, except for brewing – there were eight breweries in the town, and 'Dumfarlin yale' was held in high repute, even if many bewailed their inability to buy it. An old song commemorates this: 'As I sat near the Spittel crosshead, Dumfarlin I thocht on, An' o' its guid broon ale tae sell, But siller I had none!' This photograph shows one of the best-known brewers, James Brown. The premises became Craig's Brewery, then MacPherson's bookshop. *(DCL)*

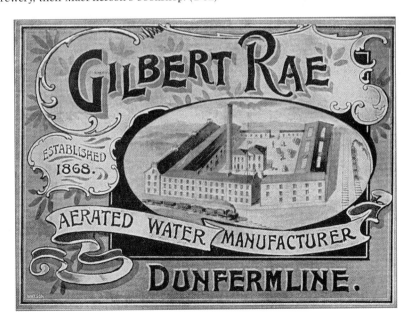

Of course not everyone took the demon drink. Gilbert Rae's aerated waters were also justly famous. This advert is taken from an early promotional booklet. *(DCL)*

Rae's Aerated Water started production in 1868 and moved to The Barracks in Golfdrum Street in 1874. The company also made ice; this ice lorry was photographed in the 1920s. Rae's Baldridge works were an early user of electric power – from 1888 the works were lit by dynamo. *(DCL)*

The crating and packing operation at Gilbert Rae's Baldridge works. *(DCL)*

Gilbert Rae wasn't the only purveyor of fizzy water. Bissett's Lemonade occupied the Glen Works in Pittencrieff Street, seen here in about 1942. The names of the staff are given as: Dodd Donaldson, Flora Swan, Sally McCluskey, Agnes Davidson, Mary MacDonald, a mystery lady, Mary Smith, Cissy Dick, Mary Robinson, Bob Wilson, Pete Mackey and, in the front, Billy Meldrum. Rae's also sold Bulmer's cider. *(DCL)*

Mitchell's, another aerated waters company, moved from Carnegie Drive in 1970, the year this picture was taken, to the new industrial estate at Touch. *(MA DCL)*

Above: Dunfermline was home to many other trades besides weaving and drinks manufacture. Rope manufacture was one. Thomas A. Buncle & Co.'s Holyrood Roperie caught fire on 12 June 1936. It was rebuilt and opened again a year later. *(DCL)*

Fife, of course, is the home of golf and the cunningly named St Andrews Golf Co. had its premises in Headwell Road. *(DCL)*

Many Dunfermline men worked on the construction of the Forth Bridge. When it opened on 4 March 1890 it was the longest railway bridge in the world and the first large structure made of steel. More than a mile long, it is higher than the dome of St Peter's in Rome. It crosses the wide Firth of Forth near Dunfermline and is one of the great engineering triumphs of Victorian Britain. Some late Victorians resisted the march of technology – William Morris said it was 'the supremest specimen of all ugliness'. Benjamin Baker, its designer, replied that its beauty lay in its functional elegance and added, 'The Eiffel Tower is a foolish piece of work, ugly, ill-proportioned and of no real use to anyone.' So there! *(DPG)*

Industry needs power, and people need heat and light, so gas delivery was itself an industry. In 1829 the Dunfermline Gas Company opened in Priory Lane. It was taken over by the town council in 1896 and the new site, shown here, opened in 1907. The Gas Works was closed in March 1969 just after this photograph was taken. *(MA/DCL)*

Normand & Thomson's engineering business started in 1905 and moved to Rumblingwell in 1921. The company's coppersmith works and brass foundry in Chalmers Street, seen here in 1925, ran out of fuel during the miners' strike the following year. Normand & Thomson's sank a shallow mine of its own at Shallowdrum to provide fuel. *(DCL)*

Laundry was also a major employer of female labour, as here at Brown's, *c.* 1930. *(DCL)*

Hill's laundry, like Brown's, employed mostly female labour, but men van drivers and delivery boys based at the Halbeath Road premises collected from and delivered to locations all over the district. Notice the three-digit phone number! *(DCL)*

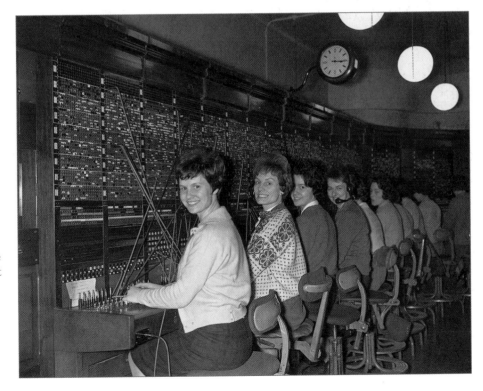

The other great employer of female labour was the telephone exchange, seen here in 1962. It was estimated, just before digital exchanges were invented, that potentially every female school leaver in the UK could become a 'telephone girl' if the uptake of phones continued as predicted. *(MA DCL)*

Mill Street was widened in about 1930. John Jackson & Sons is on the right. *(DCL)*

Jackson's coachbuilding works in Pittencrieff Street. Jackson built buses for the Scottish General Omnibus Company of Dunfermline (later taken over by Alexander's, which is now part of the Stagecoach empire). *(DCL)*

War

At Benachie House (page 67) many a thirsty serviceman was grateful for a YMCA cuppa. This was the wartime use for the Carnegie Music Institute. It is doubtful that many of the squaddies got the benefit of the 'secret bathroom'. This had been installed by the then owner, William Robertson, linen maker, in anticipation of a visit by Prime Minister Ramsay MacDonald in 1920. He never came, so he never went. *(DCL)*

Scrap metal collection 'for Spitfires' – how much of the aluminium, not to mention the miles of iron railings, collected this way ever went into aircraft or weapons manufacture is debatable. But it was a PR coup that got everyone behind the war effort. *(DCL)*

Less successful were gas masks. Almost 40 million were distributed in 1938 but after months of gas-free war, they tended to be ignored or forgotten even though it was illegal to be without a mask at any time when outdoors. *(DCL)*

The Royal Observer Corps No. 36 Group had a vital job to do, given the strategic importance of the Forth Bridge and the naval dockyards. *(DCL)*

RAF Donibristle airfield opened in 1917 as a base for the Royal Naval Air Service. In 1930 it was the home of the famous 100 Squadron, the RAF's first night bomber unit. This became No. 100 (Torpedo-Bomber) Squadron, flying Hawker Horsleys, in 1933 but the next year the squadron moved out to Singapore. During the Second World War it was known as HMS Merlin and was the Royal Naval Aircraft Repair Yard. Donibristle was also the original wartime home of the 860 (Dutch) Squadron, Fleet Air Arm. After the war it became HMS Cochrane, but closed in 1959 and the area was converted into Hillend and Donibristle industrial estates. This picture dates from 1930–3. *(DPG)*

Rosyth dock by war artist Sir Muirhead Bone (1876–1953). Bone was born in Glasgow and studied architecture and art at the Glasgow School of Art. He specialized in etching and engraving, especially of architectural subjects. An ardent nationalist, he was Britain's first official war artist during the First World War. His drawings of the Battle of the Somme, and later ruined towns and villages, were important in shaping the public mood. He was knighted in 1937. He fulfilled a similar role in the Second World War, concentrating on shipyards and battleships. *(DPG)*

VE Day, 8 May 1945, and the town is suitably bedecked, but strangely quiet. *(DCL)*

Below: A memorial for those who fell in the Second World War was erected in Monastery Street, near the First World War memorial. *(DCL)*

Growth and Change

Pitreavie Cottages, shown in this 1905 postcard, were typical of agricultural workers' tied accommodation. *(DCL)*

Before the rise of retail parks, superstores and out-of-town complexes, the Co-op – always more a way of life than just a business – took its mission seriously. The branch in Shamrock Street, off Townhill Road, used the opportunity provided by the 1951 window dressing competition to stress quality, progress, socialism and – of course – the Divvy. In case anybody is wondering, semola is still alive and kicking, although now the Italian durum wheat flour is a speciality product! *(DCL)*

The same messages can be seen on the 1911 Co-op Jubilee float, seen here in Park Place. The gents department claimed that buying a Co-op suit would produce sufficient savings to pay the rent increase. This was a time when clothes and rent were paid weekly and 'shilling a week men' collected on behalf of credit drapers and other businesses. *(DCL)*

These bungalows still stand in Aberdour Road. It is possible that they are being connected to the new gas main in this 1926 photograph. *(DCL)*

Aberdour Road, once a leafy suburban street as seen above, was developed after the war into much-needed housing, shown here under construction in 1951. This trend continues, with new, private estates emerging further east, and superstores, leisure complexes and other services appearing to cater for them. *(DCL)*

109

In a way the nineteenth century really only finished in the 1950s. The accession of a new, young queen, an ardent modernist, changed the nature of Britain irrevocably. In June 1953 like many other cinemas the Regal was showing a full-length documentary of the coronation, *A Queen is Crowned*. Special showings were organised for schoolchildren at 9*d* (about 4p) each. *(DCL)*

Dunfermline Athletic (the Pars), founded in 1885, won the Scottish Cup in 1961 under the legendary Jock Stein (front row, right), sent to Dunfermline by Celtic to learn his trade. Stein's untimely death in 1986, just as Scotland qualified for the World Cup in Mexico, affected Dunfermline football fans as much as any in Scotland. The club started as an offshoot of Dunfermline Cricket Club and played at the original East End Park, about 100 yards from the present stadium. *(DCL)*

The crowds heading down Appin Crescent for the football in 1965 were ably assisted by PC Robertson. His uniform – and his duties – were a far cry from those of his colleagues thirty years previously *(below)*. *(DCL)*

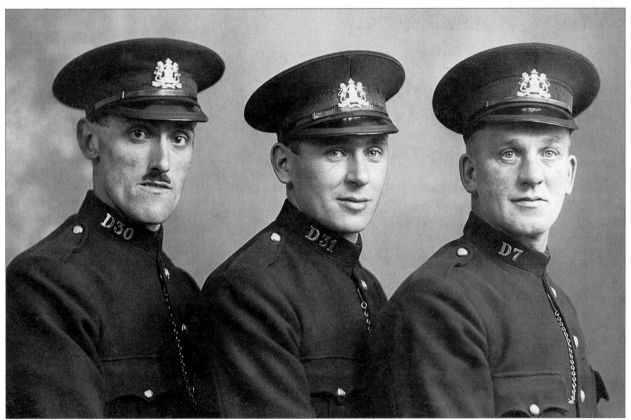

A lot of Dunfermline's expansion took place in the Abbeyview area. The brand spanking new Co-op in this 1958 photograph was a necessity. *(DCL)*

The Scottish Special Housing Association built many houses, including these at Don Road and Tweed Street. *(DCL)*

These three-storey flats in Bute Crescent were typical of the post-war social housing expansion. *(MA DCL)*

Private estates, like Garvock, also started to spring up in the 1970s. *(DCL/DPG)*

In 1962, before the rather complex roundabout was built at the beginning of Appin Crescent, the old rope works can be seen on the right, opposite the Carnegie Halls. The Girl Guide parade is turning in to St Margaret's Drive. *(DCL)*

Thomson's drapery in Holyrood Place was demolished to make way for road improvements after this 1972 photograph was taken. *(DCL)*

Holyrood Place in 1972 – they tore down a pub to build a police station, which is either a victory of a sort or a great shame, depending on your point of view. Below, the new police headquarters is under construction in 1972. *(DCL)*

Market Street, seen here in about 1960, no longer exists. It ran left before the bridge at the foot of Townhill Road where the police HQ now stands (page 115). *(DCL)*

Also long gone are many small shops like James Drylie's newsagents in Townhill Road, seen here around 1930. The shop later became R & M Aitken. *(DCL)*

In place of small shops, retail complexes came to predominate. The Kingsgate Shopping Centre was constructed in the years 1983 to 1985 as a new retail site for Dunfermline. In the process, the Opera House, Goodall's garage and the Union Inn disappeared, as did Inglis Street and Queen Anne Street. However, the new development did make use of some of their features – carved stones from the Great Fire of 1624 and the gate from the Dick's Co-operative Institutions building (page 47) are incorporated into its fabric. *(DCL)*

Dunfermline Upper Station was demolished to make way for B&Q. The station's dilapidated state can be seen in this 1988 photograph. *(DCL/Chris Seath)*

By 1989 the site had been cleared and construction of the new retail park was well under way. *(DCL)*

Dunfermline has become home to many new service businesses, replacing manufacturing as a major employer. The Bank of Scotland headquarters in Bothwell Street, with new flats behind, is shown here in 1999. *(DCL)*

Perhaps the greatest change in the twentieth century was not the shape of the town but the fabric of society. The local nobility in Dunfermline is the Bruce family, Earls of Elgin and Kincardine. This luncheon party at Broomhall in 1923 shows Queen Mary sitting between Lord and Lady Elgin. Behind her is Provost Norval, next to King George V and the Duke of York (later George VI). Holding the hand of the baby, Lady Jean Bruce, is the Duchess of York, later the Queen Mother. Mrs Louise Carnegie, who wore black after her husband's death in 1919, is seated on the far left. The present Earl has adapted nicely, taking an active role in local and national affairs and supporting the town where and when he can. *(DCL)*

Inverkeithing and Rosyth

Inverkeithing in 1895. This town of around 6,000 inhabitants is some 4 miles from Dunfermline and sits in the shadow of the Forth Bridges. Agricola, Roman Governor of Britain, is believed to have set up a camp here between AD 78 and 87. Until 1975 Inverkeithing was one of the oldest royal burghs in Scotland by virtue of charters from William the Lion in 1139 and Robert III in 1399. These included the right to hold fairs, giving the town a certain importance, character and independence. Of the five annual fairs the only one to survive is the August Lammas Fair. Local government reorganisation in the 1970s added the burgh to Dunfermline District. (A further reorganisation in 1996 put Inverkeithing directly under the control of Fife Council.) However, in its death throes Inverkeithing Town Council managed some excellent modern architecture – the Civic Centre, the library, the High School and the Ballast Bank (a sports track and leisure area, built on land reclaimed from the sea). It also preserved the character of historic buildings such as the fifth-century St Peter's Church founded by St Erat, a follower of St Ninian; the Mercat Cross (*c.* 1400); the Friary (now a local museum); the Scottish Baronial style Fordell Lodging, home of the Hendersons, Hereditary Provosts of Inverkeithing; the 1770 Town House; and Thomsoun's House (1617) with its caphoused stair tower. The medieval walls were demolished in the sixteenth century. The building which is now the Royal Hotel in the High Street (where the horse and cart are standing in the picture) was the birthplace in 1735 of Samuel Greig, 'The Father of the Russian Navy'. A cottage in Heriot Street was the childhood home of the Scottish missionary Robert Moffat, the first man to translate the Bible into an African language and father-in-law of David Livingstone. *(DPG)*

The only sizeable industries in Inverkeithing are Caldwell's paper mill (above, situated here since the 1800s and now part of the Inveresk Group), plus quarrying and shipbreaking at Jamestown. The small Belleknowes industrial park at the edge of the town provides employment, as do the larger industrial estates in neighbouring Hillend, Donibristle and Dunfermline. The former Donibristle colliery suffered a mining disaster in August 1901 when eight miners died, trapped under Moss Morran. There is no mining left and the nearby Donibristle village, once a township of 600 houses, has virtually disappeared. The proximity of the Forth Road Bridge and good rail access to Edinburgh has provided work for many locals in the capital, but has also attracted incomers with consequent house price rises. *(DCL)*

Caldwell's paper mill suffered a disastrous fire on 24 May 1913. *(DCL)*

The importance of Ward's shipbreaking yard in Jamestown, Inverkeithing, is clear from this 1971 photograph. The vessels shown are the Type 15 frigate HMS *Relentless* (built originally as a destroyer at John Brown, Clydeside, in 1942); HMS *Wakeful* (built by Fairfield of Govan in 1943, also as a destroyer but later converted to a frigate); and the submarine HMS *Ambush*. The *Mauretania* also finished her life here. (DCL)

Inverkeithing's main line railway station made it popular as a commuter town, handy for Edinburgh. However, most of the housing expansion has taken place just along the coast in Dalgety Bay. An estate long owned by the Abbots of Inchcolm, the property fell at the Reformation to Sir James Stuart of Doune whose son, the 'Bonny' Earl of Moray, was killed on the seashore below the castle in 1592. The Moray Estates sold the land to developers in the 1960s for the purpose of creating a new town, shown here in its early development. There are now 3,000 homes and a population nearing 15,000. Donibristle House can be seen at the lower left and the inset postcard shows it in more detail. It was rebuilt after a fire in 1858 and again in 1998, but reflects the style of the 1790 Georgian original. (DPG; inset BD)

121

Rosyth is well known as a naval dockyard, but it is not generally realized that it was Scotland's first – and only – garden suburb. The original 1916 plan to build 3,000 houses was cut back to about 150. The back of this postcard bears the somewhat bucolic description probably intended to encourage settlers: 'Rosyth Village . . . has been built by Messrs. Easton Gibb & Son, the contractors for the naval base at Rosyth. The climate is dry, healthy and bracing. It is a complete community in itself and has a Church, Reading Room, Tea-Room, Canteen, Grocery and Provision Stores, Bakery, recreation and football grounds etc. It is electrically lighted and each Habitation has a good water supply. Food is cheap and rents are low. Swings and different kinds of amusements are provided for the children, and Cinematographic Entertainments, Band performances, etc. are given regularly.' Well, who wouldn't want to live there, eh? *(DPG)*

Some of the roads in 'Rosyth Garden City' had suitably Fabian names – this crater appeared in Bernard Shaw Street in 1956. However, the prefabs were known locally as 'Tin Town'. Rosyth has a longer history than its twentieth-century flowering would suggest. The ruins of Rosyth Castle, once a huge edifice, stand on a promontory about 2 miles along the coast from North Queensferry and 4 miles south of Dunfermline. At high water it was entirely surrounded, as if on its own island. The main structure is of the Norman keep type, high and with thick walls. The main door to the north side has an armorial stone dated 1561 (the year of construction) and bearing the initials MR (Maria Regina). A large window on the east side is marked 1655, the date of repairs necessary after Cromwell's men did it significant damage. *(MA DCL)*

This tram at 'Tin Town', Rosyth, shows how to turn a necessity into a virtue. None of the Dunfermline trams could have roofs as the Halbeath Road bridges were too low, so 'garden' seats were used on the top deck. *(DCL)*

In 1903 the Admiralty decided to capitalize on the tide-free bay and established a naval base and royal dockyard. HMS *Zealandia* was the first ship to enter Rosyth lock on 27 March 1916. But Rosyth had always been a good berth. It is not absolutely clear where Edgar the Ætheling, his mother, sisters and courtiers disembarked after their ship arrived in the Forth (page 13), but it is likely to have been near where Rosyth Castle later stood, the bay afterwards known as St Margaret's Hope, 4 miles south of Malcolm's Tower. The name Rosyth itself does not appear until the late 1300s but may stem from the Gaelic word *ross* (a promontory or peninsula) and the Anglo-Saxon *hythe* (a landing place, as in Rotherhithe and Hythe in Kent) or possibly the Gaelic *saighead* (arrow). The bay is certainly more sheltered from storms and east winds than other possible landing places, and even the nineteenth-century poet Mercer says it is: '. . . a sheltered, safe retreat, For tempest-driven vessels meet'. *(DPG)*

The Navy leaves. Feelings ran high towards the end of the twentieth century when it was announced that Rosyth's naval base would lose out to Devonport, Plymouth, for the contract to refit Trident submarines. In 1991 the Conservative government, having invested about £120 million in the Rosyth facility, suddenly announced a review. *Inset*: Local support for Rosyth's continued role as a dockyard was intense in the early 1990s. The banner is a reference to the seven nuclear submarines scrapped at Rosyth and likely to stay there well into the next millennium. *(DPG)*

In 1993 defence secretary Malcolm Rifkind, conscious that the Conservatives were losing ground to the Liberal Democrats in the sensitive south-west of England, announced that Devonport had won the contract to refit Trident submarines. Over 4,000 Rosyth jobs, plus all the associated employment, were at stake. The promise of 'allocated work' for surface ships never materialized. Even with an impressive array of national and local support, local MPs Gordon Brown and Rachel Squire could not influence the decision. A massive foundation hole in the ground the size of thirty football pitches was the only memorial to what might have been. Investment by Babcock, which acquired Rosyth as Britain's first privatized dockyard in 1997, provided employment for some 2,000, but it looked like Rosyth's naval heyday was truly over. *(DPG)*

Then the political tide turned. By 2000 the Labour government was in power, Scotland had some devolved autonomy and Gordon Brown was Chancellor of the Exchequer with Dr Lewis Moonie, MP for neighbouring Kirkcaldy, at the Department of Defence. Devonport was judged to have performed badly on Trident – going over time and over budget – and didn't have sufficient docking. The aircraft carriers *Ark Royal*, *Invincible* and *Illustrious* were scheduled for refits in 2001 and 2002 and it became increasingly likely that two 1,000-foot super carriers might be assembled, fitted out and maintained at Rosyth. Apart from the jobs boost, this would secure the future of nearby HMS Caledonia, an important naval shore station and support centre, and the Defence Munitions plant at Crombie. *(DPG)*

Acknowledgements

The author owes a great debt of gratitude to: the staff of the Local History Centre, Dunfermline Carnegie Library, including Dorothy Miller, Sharron McColl, Helen Penman and especially Chris Neale, that necessary man; the Dunfermline Press Group – Mrs Deirdre Romanes for her tolerance and Bill Livingstone for his wisdom; Bev, Ronnie and Nazareth (rock on, guys!); Lee Melville of Inveresk Plc; the burghers of Dunfermline Toun itself, who didn't mind a Kirkcaldy man writing about them; and to Natasha who walked it with me and fell in love with the place.

PICTURE CREDITS

Images marked as DCL are the property and copyright of Dunfermline Carnegie Library and used here with their permission. Images marked MA DCL are part of the Morris Allen Archive at Dunfermline Carnegie Library. Images marked DPG are the property and copyright of the Dunfermline Press Group and used here with its permission. Other illustrations are either in the public domain or belong to the author. Postcards used in the book have been donated to Dunfermline Carnegie Library by the author as a small token of a big appreciation.

The image of Canmore's Tower is on the town arms today, seen here on the Provost's Lamp. At one time provosts and bailies (senior councillors) had special gas lamps erected outside their houses so the public could identify them. As in other Scottish towns, this practice passed into history with the abolition of the burghs in the 1990s. *(DPG)*